"Mx. Evergreen paints the harrowing in the colors of the mundane, and makes the mundane all the more harrowing for it. Ze expresses the hardest times of zir life with a seemingly effortless clarity that can only come from years of work to understand zirself. This is sharp, tense autobiographical storytelling coming from the safe hindsight of growth and love, and I reach the end wonderstruck."

~Joy Redcedars, *radix.nekoweb.org*

"There's a terrible magic in this book that turns it into a mirror. I see myself in the desperation, the hunger, and the longing. This book is not just about a cat. It's about the author, and it's about the reader."

~Nathaniel Luscombe, author of *My Roots Can't Leave the Ground*

"*Best Cat in Show* is a timely, poignant collection. Sage Evergreen writes like a creature possessed by a story bigger than themself, blunt and sharp and gentle, all at once. Erelah Emerson's illustrations elevate this brilliant tale to new heights, as Evergreen takes a chisel and hammer to xir life, fashioning the pain of surveillance, loneliness, and longing, into a hard-fought story of trans survival. The cat does not die in this book, and I love xim for it."

~MJ Anthony, author of *Tending Clay; Unearthing Stars*

BEST CAT IN SHOW

sage evergreen also appears in:

There is Us: a covid-19 anthology
Faces to the Sun: a mental health anthology

also from Dragon Heart Press

Unleash the Cosmos: A Space Poetry Anthology
When One World Ends, Another Begins
by Nathaniel Luscombe
Tending Clay; Unearthing Stars by MJ Anthony
ThistleHeart Home by R.C. Lloyd

best cat in show

sage evergreen

Published in Hackett, Arkansas USA by Dragon Heart Press,
an imprint of Dragon Bone Publishing™ LLC 2025.

Cover created by and copyright of Effie Joe Stock.
Interior formatting by MJ Anthony.
Interior illustrations by Erelah Emerson.

to the cats, old and new. to the dog, who i love. and to the judges, who performed a miracle for a scared cat.

-sage

Content warnings:
self harm, medical neglect, emotional abuse, suicidal ideation

Schedule of Events

participant's laurels: a mini-collection

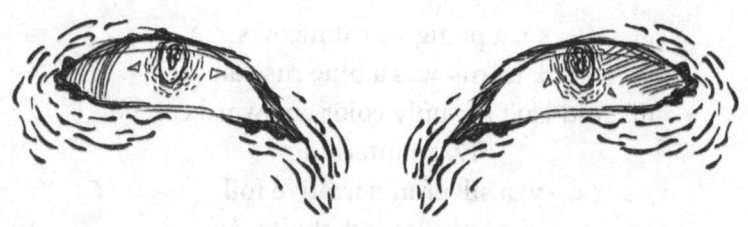

i. a pedigree cat meows

the thing about being a cat bred for competition
is that your life is no longer your own
and even though you have strange dreams about running
through forests
far away from groomers and medals and floodlight eyes
doesn't every cat?
it doesn't mean anything
that your breath catches upon waking
that there is a terror you cannot explain
dropping into the pit of your stomach
not when you are chased by a fox
but when your handlers pet you
you are such a good girl, they say
something in your jaw aches at this praise
teeth that have never torn into anything harder than the
food pellets they give you
at least you are not the dog
barking and snarling but always, always
eventually giving in
(through this you learn one thing- the will of a handler is
absolute.)

ii. icarus was a blue russian

the first time you stumble in a competition
is passed off as a fluke by your handlers
no one but the dog sees you as you tend to yourself
her smile stuffed with teeth and malice
but you know not to break eye contact.
(never break eye contact with a threat/judge/handler)
but it happens more and more
the dreams following you into the arena
you bite yourself to make them stop
hoping your handlers won't notice
but the will of a handler is inevitable
(a handler is inevitable)
and they still let you compete
but you get muzzled after you leave the arena
no amount of thrashing will take it off
you have watched the dog try
and so
despite the pine trees rippling under your fur
you stay still
stay a perfect specimen for the judges
and eventually the muzzle comes off
no one the wiser
except for perhaps the dog
(hard to hide something you both hold in common.)

iii. gold isn't the only color an award can be

here's the thing about the dog
she doesn't compete like you do
not the prettiest in show
no, the dog does different competitions
ones where her teeth come in handy
the handlers treat her roughly
and she in turn does the same
you think
if you were less quiet
less good at being handled
that they would make you do what the dog does
but you do not hate the dog
even when it looks like her teeth might get turned on you
(even when she rattles your cage)
because the benefit of having a tentative position
as the pampered pet
means you understand exactly what will happen
should you fail to win every ribbon you can
the dog, on the other hand
only knows the blood of a good fight
victory ripped out with her teeth and claws
you do not fault the dog for this
(that does not mean that sometimes you are not afraid of
the dog.)

iv. an interlude

you remember a time
before the competitions
before the medals
(before the dreams of hunter green and a heady wood
smell)
when you were allowed to bask in the sunlight every once
in a while
the dog was still harsh, true
but sometimes she would lie down with you
curl into your side
she was only a puppy then
and neither of you knew what was to come
you remember watching the stray cats come into your
yard
hunting birds and all sorts of other creatures
and sometimes you would join them
(the fence always large enough to keep you inside)
but you were always careful to lick away any blood
important, for reasons you didn't yet understand
it felt safe in those lazy summer afternoons
in a way you never knew
until that safety was gone
until the medals and the judges crowded out anything
else
you don't miss it
not because it wasn't pleasant
but because you cannot afford mistakes
(is it a mistake to long for peace?)

v. a silver in narrative foil

at the next competition
you see a curious cat
an abyssinian that hisses and snarls at the judges
that receives the lowest score you've ever seen
and yet, you cannot take your eyes off of her
perhaps for the sheer novelty
of a champion cat that fights back
her build is lanky, and her eyes scour the room
like each handler has wronged her somehow
you watch as her handler
whispers furiously to her
but every competition that comes after
you watch for her
every competition
her point score only improves marginally
it seems that she will never be tamed
you do not approach her
because you know what your handlers would do
but from her you learn a small spark of defiance
a seed planted in your pouch
(she reminds you of the dreams, of running through
forests, of freedom)

vi. the jaws that bite

the abyssinian is not the only new cat
a maine coon with broad shoulders and a dense coat
swans in
new to this circuit, of course
but an old favorite with the judges
he's got the finest groomers
and a handler that watches the other cats like a hawk
when you are alone
(alone enough – a show cat is never unwatched)
he speaks with you gently
he smells like something you have never experienced
before
it is only when he gets closer
puts his teeth around your neck like a new kind of collar
that you realize the smell is noxious artificial pine
and that he has not been outside in a very long while
(he is a favorite of the judges. what did you think would
happen?)

vii. moggy competition

you cannot rid your mind of the dreams
they come in heavy, wrapping you up
in the scent of trees and grass and foxes
of a freedom you have never been allowed
even in the soft cocoon of summer
so you stumble in competition
your handlers scowling
and they trace your gaze
to the abyssinian
(*no*)
you do not see her again
not when your handlers can help it
you are scooped away whenever she is in the vicinity
the competitions change
and you are entered into arenas where you could win in a
heartbeat
you do not complain
because there is something your handlers never
considered
a different arena means different cats
means a different competition circuit
means a chance to breathe in hunter green
even if it is artificial
it hums with the frequency of your dreams
you do not let your handlers know
and you are once again
perfect in show
(but now, you know something they don't.)

viii. the elysian fields are filled with mixed breed charmers

there is a sort of joy
in being able to compete with house cats
you have been so used to a strict diet, a rigid exercise
that to see other cats with their owners
is a release of air that you didn't know you'd been holding
they nudge up against you
curl around you like the dog used to
and you find that you want to protect them
(you could not protect the dog.)
your handlers are absent in these competitions
they know you know what to do
you have watched the dog often enough
to know that you must be cautious
but even with that knowledge
you find your diet loosening
the other cats a comforting pile
instead of competitors to be watched out for
you ease into these competitions
careful, still, ever cautious
but it becomes a place where you can relax
an arena that does not immediately raise your hackles
judges that gloss over mistakes
that would have been an immediate disqualification before
all of this means
that you let your guard down enough
to realize that perhaps you do not want to compete
anymore
(a foolish idea, as you will see)

ix. the claws that do not catch

there is only one meeting that truly scares you
you meet with another pedigree cat
one who almost broke out of the circuit
who had the dreams of forest and moss green
of pine tree smell
but really, he knows that's wrong now
a pedigree cat should be obedient
should be lovely
should behave
after all, isn't this what we were bred for?
is this not what we have trained for?
when he smiles, you see his teeth are the perfect size for
his breed
no smaller, no larger
they fit frighteningly well in his skull
never used to bite
only ever used to smile
do you think that if they applied enough pressure
locked the doors of the arena
that you would become like him?
he stretches before you leave
and you watch his paws
(the nails are clipped down to a nub)

You Remember the Dog

x. pedigree judges at a moggy competition

the thing about moggy competitions though
is that there's always someone willing to judge you
your handlers pull you away one cold night
and watch you eat
they are disgusted with how insubordinate you have
become
bring you to groomers, to trainers, to anyone who might
be able to fix you
and you curse the thought that you could have been safe
anywhere
there are owners that are watching you, they say
and suddenly no one is safe
not the housecats you once considered friends
not the judges who were so kind to you
they make you visit a pedigree judge
who hems and haws about proper feeding habits
about how being around housecats has made you weak
after all, what good is a show cat without a pleasant
attitude?
you visit another who tells you that the dreams of forests
will all go away
the second you begin to compete in the pedigree level
again
and even though you know they're wrong
you also know that it is dangerous to defy them
even though nothing has happened yet
(you remember the dog. you remember the dog. you
remember the dog.)

xi. an agreement on a tie

the thing about being a pedigree cat once
is that it never slips out from underneath your fur
the ability to be best in show never fades from your
muscles
even when it fades from your mind
your handlers begin to plan your next competition
pedigree only, of course
they'll let you stay in the moggy competitions for a while
on the agreement that this desire to not compete anymore
was only a fluke
just like when you tried to bite yourself
you slipped and made a mistake
and this desire to no longer be a pedigree cat
well, we all make mistakes, don't we?
they know that you love competitions
that you'll come back over to their side
that you never wanted to make them unhappy
what cat would be so cruel?
you are a pedigree cat
the finest in your region
and so they send you back into the moggy competitions
but here's the thing about being a pedigree cat
it does not stop you from making your own plans
(handlers may be inevitable, but that does not mean that
yours have to be)

xii. outstanding circumstances

then, something you don't expect
a way out, if you perform correctly
please all the right judges, your markings gleaming in the
sunlight
your handlers are confused, but if you preen just right
they might not even notice
you must be more cautious
more cunning than you have ever been
but if you did not know how to lie
then you wouldn't have made it to moggies in the first
place
the housecats you trust more than anything help you
the judges who have been kind deflect questions
sometimes
and after all
what cat wouldn't want a last hurrah tour
before they go back to pedigree competitions?
clever little kitty
make sure that your handlers do not notice
the way that your pupils grow thin when they speak to
you
make sure that they do not notice
the undercurrent of anger in your meowing
and you may just win the best prize of all
(dreams of the forest becoming reality.)

xiii. the forest beckons

you knew the other shoe would drop sometimes, though
your handler screaming at you from the other side of the
phone
(and she's the nice one, you know)
but strangely
the judges do not comply
they wrap you up in a warm blanket
send you off to a place your handler does not know of
and while you no longer have a groomer or a trainer
the forest is now yours to explore
freedom, it turns out, tastes a lot like terrible wet food
but you gobble down every bite
fascinated with every new sensation
as much as you are terrified
the will of a handler is inevitable (?)
but for now, you are safe
for now, you can play with the housecats
hunt mice and other little crawling things
choke them down with kitty kibble
the kind that you were never allowed to have before
and while the forest is scary
it is also freeing to be able to be frightened
to not have to hold it in your stomach while your
handlers
smiled
(nothing lasts forever, but does it have to last forever to be
wonderful?)

xiv. breed standards for the cream point birman

only, here's the thing about being a pedigree
you'll always be valuable to someone
as a pedigree, of course
prized for competition
or for your ovaries, to create
a new litter of champions
(don't look so scared- you should be grateful, honored)
and even as you run through the forest
your handler is coming for you
after all, isn't the will of a handler inevitable?
how fast can you run, little kitty cat
how clever can you be?
your handler is 322 miles away
but that distance is rapidly closing
if your handler goes 58 miles per hour
with a gas break inbetween
and you stand still in fear
how long will it take for your handler to reach you
tear the forest out of you
and bring you back to competition where you belong
(calculate quickly, little kitty cat- this is a timed test)

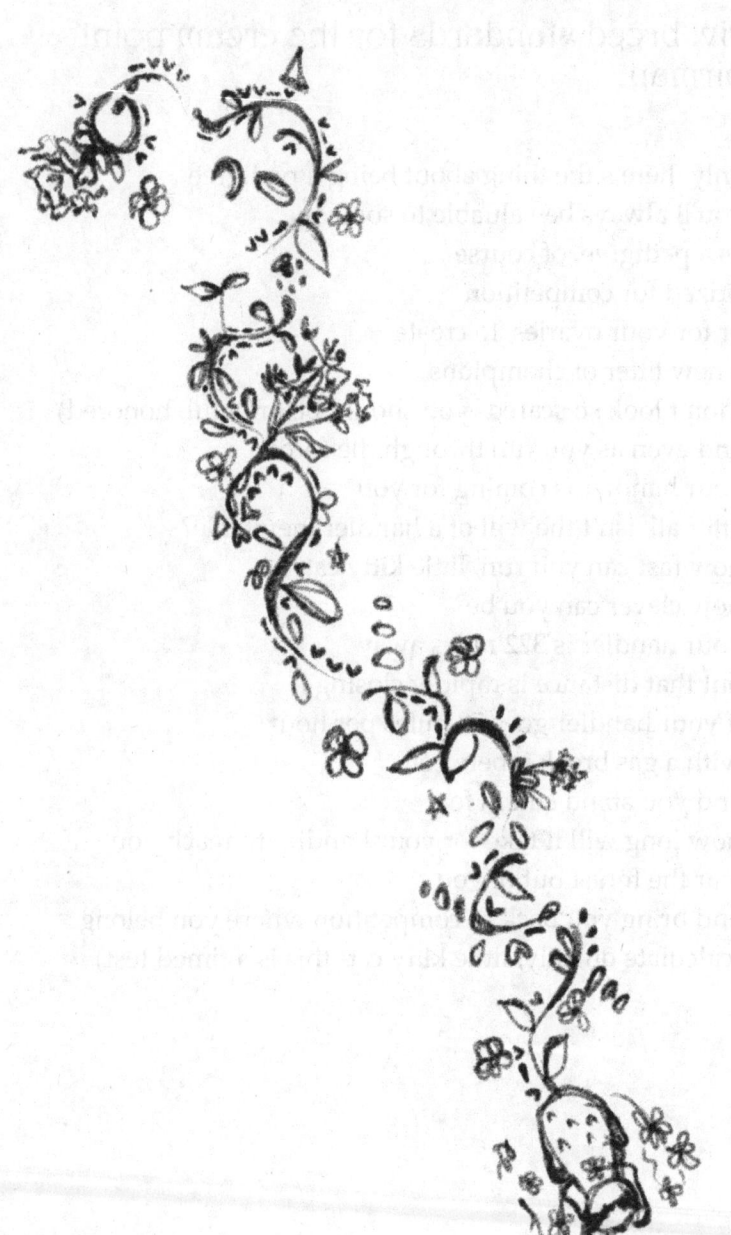

xv. the vote has been recalled

pedigree cats are not bred to run
pedigree cats are bred to look pretty
pedigree cats are bred to win competitions
but you are not a pedigree cat anymore
and you find yourself ill-suited to being hunted
shaking like a leaf in your den
what worries you so, little kitty-cat
is it your handler, stomping about
in the moggies
in the judges' houses
wailing that someone has stolen her prize kitten
or is it something else
are you worried that when your handler finds you
your jaw will not open
you will not be able to bite or snarl or even hiss
but instead, little kitty cat
you will go quietly to the last competition
hoping to find a car to collide with
hoping the housecats will forgive you
you and i both know the truth, little kitty-cat
(lying to yourself is a waste of time you cannot afford)

xvi. bred for aesthetics

even if you are no longer a pedigree cat in competition
you still have the body of a pedigree cat
your bones or muscles or joints
aching under the weight of you
and maybe
just maybe
when you stumbled it was not your fault
so when you stumble in the next competition
there is no handler to blame you
and when you go to the vet
they examine you with a caution
so gentle it alarms you
and when they let you know that your pain is not normal
it feels better than every award you still have
when they give you a specialized doctor
the forest flows through you
and you have been released from a burden
you didn't know you were carrying
(a hallelujah to a god you don't believe in, like an exhale)

xvii. here comes the drop

and in five minutes
or less
they tell you what's wrong
the pain and shame and guilt of
eight *years*
over in one appointment
so simple
it feels like your handlers could have done it
(it feels like your handlers *should* have done it)
but the doctor sends you off
a prescription for a medication
to be wrapped in whatever food you'll swallow
isn't it funny
one little blue pill
once at bedtime
and the pain lifts a little
easy as a summer afternoon
you see, the pain isn't in your bones
or your muscles
or your joints
it's your nerves that are the problem
or your nervous system, to be more specific
kitty-cat, it is not your fault
kitty-cat, they say it may be genetic
kitty-cat, they say it may be the trauma
(you think you know why your handlers didn't fix it)

xviii. reunion tour

you sit in front of your handler
tail swishing back and forth, anxious/angry coloring your
body
her hands are folded neatly in front of her
like she can pretend her way into normalcy
like she is visiting a beloved housecat
that simply had to be placed in a different house
a shame! we won't think about it further
your fur has a few leaves stuck in it
some fresh blood from a kill this morning
and she stares openly at it while you chirp
about the birds you have seen and the cats you have
hunted with
you are not the cat she handled anymore
not so easily cowed into obedience
there lies a ring of trophies around your neck
vole teeth and rabbit tails
it moves as you breath, easy as a spring breeze
even as you think
about how thoroughly you cloaked yourself in forest
greens
(how did she find you, hiding in the brush?)

xix. genetic trauma

the doctors have given you words now
and you tell your handler
about how the creaking of your bones may be
your lineage
your breeding
an important thing for her to know, of course
(you think of the dog)
she is quiet when she tells you that no
she has never heard bones creak like yours
in the others
like branches in a strong wind
she is, sorry, of course
the same way everyone who does not know is
it feels different, though
an ax rested and rusting on the stump of a great old tree
not enough to undo the hurt it caused
wounds leaking into each other
you wonder, in the cool of the night
if you are truly the first of your lineage to have bones that
sway
(the ax has a wooden handle – was it once a tree too?)

xx. a kaleidoscope moves into one image

and here we are in the present
you a wooden sculpture before me
me looking you in your slitted pupils
i don't know what comes next
but i know that this is where you start/end
and where i keep going
and maybe we will see each other again
when you are dusted off
to help me work my way around
the grooves in the statue of you
the carving is a story
every stroke of the gouge an experience
that i have given to you
that we have shared together
and maybe in the sharing of the statue
we will be able to understand ourself
we will be able to share ourself
we will be able to love ourself
(growth and health and life from a place where there was
only ash before)

author's note:

i write this author's letter in a very different place than the place i wrote best cat in show from.

when i was writing, and quite frankly going through the events of best cat in show, it seemed like the future was something that i was continually preparing for. that i would eventually experience the love and affection for the person that i was, and not for the flimsy projection that i gave to others. i bottled bits of sunlight in preparation for the day that i would be able to go out into the sun, and enjoy it unafraid.

that day has come, and i could not be more glad for it.

i love being in the future more than i could possibly express. there are rainy days, of course, as there always are. but i think every moment is something greater than when i stayed inside for fear of what would happen if i strayed.

best cat in show, to me, is a testament to survival. if you find yourself in the same situation, if some of the earlier poems hit harder than the later ones, i want you to know that if you can make it, we're waiting for you. i won't claim it's easy, because that would come across as insincere, and you and i both know it won't be. but if you can find your people, they will love you if you can love them back.

for those who have made it out into the sunlight with me: congratulations. the world may spin on, but we know what it took to get us here. however you made it here, i am proud of you. you have weathered the storm. enjoy the sun.

and for my own group of moggies, those who helped me come to enjoy the light, i cannot express enough gratitude. you are the reason i am able to write this letter. may we have many more happy reunions.

whatever you take away from this collection, whoever you are: i love you. you are worth loving. you are worth being, in whatever form you like. love freely, love deeply.

PARTICIPANT'S LAURELS
(a mini collection)

start from the beginning

i have a pet i think
that isn't right. let me start over.
i have a wild beast
it follows my family
howling and baring its teeth
whenever i try to mention it
it bites my arm
with fiery jaws
it almost clasped its fangs around my neck once
people politely do not mention it.
(that isn't right. let me start over.)
i am drowning with a weight attached to my ankle
when i was younger and
kinder
i used to scream to try to get people to help me
but with every scream the weight would grow heavier
and my voice would grow hoarser
until i learned that it was better not to scream at all
and just thrash and flail
hoping to make it to the surface myself
(that isn't right. let me start over.)
i am scraping my way up from a no man's land
covered in mud and blood
that might very well be mine

was, at one point, mine
the last time i asked for help
they threw me on the front lines and said find your way
out
people who should have known better
and when i saw their faces again
they did not speak of what they had done to me
(that shouldn't be right. but it is.)

prescribed burning

the thing that people don't tell you about wildflowers
is that if you don't burn them back
they will grow over your hands and feet
cling to you and hold you down
sprout over your mouth and fill it
with beautiful petals that choke you out
so pretty to look at
(no one really cares about the lungs of pretty things)
sometimes people will give you flames
to burn away bits and pieces of the wildflowers
to grow their own instead
cactus flowers and red anemones and dead lilies
wilting you from the inside out
let your own fire out my love
curb their flowers and free yourself
keep the wildflowers out of your throat
you are not burning every field
by turning a handful of invasive flowers to ash

the sunflower cycle

i.

i had a dream last night
i was standing in a field bordered by wheat
the field itself, though, was full of black, loamy soil
and a woman, almost as dark as the soil she worked in
i asked her
where am i? what is this place?
and she told me
it's what you make of it. it's yours after all.
and when she went back to working
i saw a man standing in the wheat
looking at me with disdain
and so i went over to him
and i asked him
this tall, pale, sickly man who looked like death warmed
over,
why do you frown so? what troubles you?
and he told me
*she's wrong, you know it's not your field. it's a wheat field, and
it was meant for wheat.*
if you grow anything else there, it's wrong.
and so i went back to the woman, with her basket of
seeds
and i told her

that man said i had to plant wheat here
and she smiled softly and said
you plant what you need to plant. but i have a feeling
that wheat will strangle your field.
and i looked at my ankles and i saw
that the bone-skinny man's wheat was tangled around
them
and the woman said
it's your choice what you plant here- wheat or sunflowers
but you're gonna have to choose soon because harvest time is
coming
wheat or sunflowers, son?
and when i started to speak, i felt the earth pulling me in
and a stalk began to grow out of the top of my head
(i woke up before i could see what it was.)

ii.

i had another dream last night
i was buried in the earth
or
maybe. not buried, but planted in the dark soil
i was not scared of being in the soil, but rather
scared of what i would grow into
the soil was warm and safe and nurturing
but i remembered what the woman said
harvest time is coming
i had to choose
whether to become a sunflower or a wheat field
and i remembered what the man said
it was meant for wheat. it's not your field
and the sunflower in me shriveled a little in my chest
and the wheat rattled around my ankles
and my heart ached
because i knew what i wanted
fields of sunflowers as far as the eye could see
but i was afraid
of what the old sickly man would say
when he saw those golden yellow petals blooming out of
the field
i was scared of how he would act
when he saw my crown of sunlight

would he shun me? scowl at me? deny me?
would he pretend i'd planted wheat, like he told me i had
to?
would my sunflowers be worth that pain?
and i heard the woman saying
it's time to wake up
harvest time is here,
and what kind of crop have you chosen, my son?
and my eyes opened up under that soil
and i looked her in the eyes
and i said,
i choose sunflowers.

iii.

i had a third dream last night
i was tending my sunflowers
pruning them, watering them, weeding them
and in the distance stood the pale and sickly man
and with a dry, hacking cough, he told me
you know, wheat wouldn't take so much effort. your sunflowers
take so much time, and wouldn't it be nice to take a break?
and i told him,
my sunflowers take time, yes
but so do all crops- my sunflowers are not special in that aspect
sometimes i see sadness in his eyes
and it makes me want to tear out every sunflower
and plant in his wheat
even though my ankles still itch from where it held me
from where, in my darkest nights with no moon to guide
me, it creeps back
but i think of all the work i've done
planting my sunflowers, nurturing them
all the people who have told me
i have found joy in your sunflowers
and all the people they will bring joy to in the future
and perhaps one day
i will see the pale and sickly old man
smiling at my sunflowers

and on that day
i hope that i can tell him, without reservation,
i am glad that you like my sunflowers
would you like to see them up close?
and i hope that the old man can find the bravery
or if he can't, borrow some of mine
and say
yes, i would like that very much
but until then
i will take care of my sunflowers, and make them
beautiful
for myself, if no one else

iv.

it has been many months since i dreamed
about the old man in my garden
but the other night he came to my sunflower fields
and he started to board them up
he had put in a fence around his own wheat
so that he did not have to see my beautiful yellow petals
and i cried *enough!*
you have desecrated my garden!
leave, and do not come back!
i chased him out of my fields
and he trampled some sunflowers as he fled
but when he left my fields seemed brighter
as though banishing him brought sunlight to my fields
maybe one day he will come back
not with a hammer and boards
but with open hands and an open heart
until then, though
i will welcome the sunlight
and the rain that will come afterwards
i will welcome my new neighbors
who harvest lilacs and violets
my war is over
and i have found some peace
(hallelujah, praise be)

divinity on the side of the road

on my way home today
i saw the shell of venus
empty, and a little dirty
she'd left a long time ago
with the whispers of sunflowers in my ears
and her shell held a crown of them in its blue embrace
i put it on my head
hoping that it would not fall around my neck
and choke me out with its bright and sickly yellow
venus told me something else
to seek out someone with sunflowers in their hair
i was half tempted to search out every person with bits of
yellow sticking out of their pockets
but the thing is
that not every scrap of yellow belongs to a sunflower
you cannot wring the joy out of a simulacrum
that was never intended to hold the weight you give it
i have found some of those that venus intended for me
weaved in my sunflowers with theirs
and i think together
we are much stronger
(weave the pillars together and get something stronger
than the parts)

victory lap

and this is what life is like after the storm
christmas lights on the porch
curled up in a halloween blanket
while your dog sleeps peacefully at your feet
there are other storms
but now
you have hatches to batten down
food and water and batteries
so when the thunder rolls
and the winds howl
you have more than a few shingles to hang onto
more folks to call
more hands to hold
and shoulders to cry on
(we got through the hurricane. we made it.)

acknowledgments

there are many people without whom this book would never exist, and many more who will always remain close to my heart—but here are a sample of a few.

to my sister, bella—i wish you wealth, i wish you health, and i hope that whatever deity is listening protects you from this heinous heat. i love you.

to my roommate first, and my friend forever, ziel—it is a privilege to know you and a joy to hear about the creatures you treat on a daily basis. may your troubles be less, your blessings be more, and may we see each other face to face soon.

to micah—your friendship means more to me than i can write. i love reading your writing, and it warms my heart how much you like reading mine. may i have a thousand thousand more words for you, and may we be able to share in person soon.

to the love of my life and the light of my days, my partner in crime and other ways—i cannot believe we have been together for five years. every day you bring more joy into my life than i would have thought possible. may we have many more years together.

to nathaniel—thank you for your kind words, and for believing in *best cat* even when i could not. it is an honor to be published alongside you.

to effie—thank you for a beautiful cover that truly captures the essence of *best cat*.

to rae—thank you for your wonderful illustrations that break my heart and soothe it in the way that they understand what i was writing about.

to my beautiful baby daughter honey—you can't read this because you are a dog, but every time i look in your little eyes i feel love. i love you too, baby girl. stop eating paper.

to everyone who has read *best cat* and *participant's laurels*, and to the english club i hold forever in my heart—every word i write is for you. thank you.

and if *best cat* has resonated with you—you are seen. you are loved. we will make it through the darkness to the other side.

may it be well.

as a thank you for reading this book & purchasing
the paperback, you can download the ebook
version in our store for free!

dragonbonepublishing.gumroad.com/l/best-cat

with code:
bc3fjske-p

If you enjoyed this collection, you might like these other titles!

Tending Clay; Unearthing Stars
by MJ Anthony

Today I am learning // to take anxiety by the hand // and teach this trembling, fragile beast // that we are (and yet will be) // okay.

In their debut collection, MJ Anthony navigates a complicated web of intersecting topics such as complex trauma, neurodiversity, lasting illness, and practicing self-love in a body long-alienated from you. Alongside the reader, the author combs tangles into threads and weaves them into a gentler future, reunifying selves and stories both old and new.

Part hurting, part healing, and wholly original, *Tending Clay; Unearthing Stars* is a love letter to everyone living with a broken body or a troubled mind.

"An introspective tapestry of poetry that is as profound as it is touching."
—PEDRO INIGUEZ, Author of Mexicans on the Moon: Speculative Poetry from a Possible Future

WHEN ONE WORLD ENDS, ANOTHER BEGINS

POEMS
NATHANIEL LUSCOMBE

When One World Ends, Another Begins
by Nathaniel Luscombe

"Words became my bloodletting. I've been bleeding now for years."

At times playful, at times heartbreaking, *When One World Ends, Another Begins* is a raw, honest look at how it feels to be alive. On the surface, these poems are an examination of what it is to be human. Underneath, they're an exploration of body image, fear, faith, and the ways life runs in circles. They exist to peel back the tough layers and expose the softness inside.

About the Author

sage evergreen (xe/ze/they) was found in a fairy circle in the middle of the woods. despite the multiple efforts to make them wear iron, ze remains untamed in the realm of suburban tennessee. legend says that if you put out a full pan of stovetop stuffing and the rise and fall of a midwestern princess, you will awake with a mouthful of moss and xir most recent written words in your hands.